BOOKS BY DAVID SCHLOSS

Reports from Babylon and Beyond
Group Portrait from Hell
Behind the Eyes
Greatest Hits
Sex Lives of the Poor and Obscure
Legends
The Beloved

REPORTS FROM
BABYLON
AND BEYOND

POEMS

David Schloss

DOS MADRES
2015

DOS MADRES PRESS INC.

P.O.Box 294, Loveland, Ohio 45140
www.dosmadres.com   editor@dosmadres.com

Dos Madres is dedicated to the belief that the small press is essential
to the vitality of contemporary literature as a carrier of the new voice,
as well as the older, sometimes forgotten voices of the past. And in an
ever more virtual world, to the creation of fine books pleasing to the
eye and hand.

Dos Madres is named in honor of Vera Murphy and Libbie Hughes,
the "Dos Madres" whose contributions have made this press possible.

Dos Madres Press, Inc. is an Ohio Not For Profit Corporation and a
501 (c) (3) qualified public charity. Contributions are tax deductible.

Executive Editor: Robert J. Murphy

Illustration & Book Design: Elizabeth H. Murphy
www.illusionstudios.net

Typset in New Times Roman & American Typewriter
ISBN 978-1-939929-40-2
Library of Congress Control Number: 2015944302

First Edition

ACKNOWLEDGMENTS

I am grateful to the editors of the following publications
in which some of these poems previously appeared,
often in somewhat different versions:

Behind the Eyes, (Dos Madres Press, Cincinnati, 2005):
"Homeless Harry Sold His House."

The Cincinnati Review: "The Universe."

Flights: "A Foreign Correspondent," "Repatriation," "Song for
the New Dark Age," "State Politician Arriving Late."

Praxilla: "A Foreign Correspondent," "Secreted in Secular Orders."

Note: All unattributed quotations in the text are by the author.

CONTENTS

This book is for Signe, if she wants it.

REPORTS FROM
BABYLON
AND BEYOND

I.
Decline of the West

We happened to happen
upon their greatest works
in which they almost had
things go only their way–
but when their towers fell,
by then, so, too, had they.

.

Witnesses to Natural Events

"All was at risk with the heavens"
—Signe Schloss

1. Catching the Comet's Tail

We see, with moon-occluded eyes,
this ancient threat we can't ignore
emerging from the depths of skies
in paleness, white on black before
one body has completely covered
the other, together like two lovers,
funereal as some fresh-cut flowers
floating out upon darkened waters,
witnessing that still-emptying sky,
watching the traffic of stars go by.

2. Tsunami

Moments before big waves struck
all along those little-visited coasts,
with nothing more to resist it than
an instinct, dumb fear, dumb luck,
the tourists took a camera and ran
towards sea-floors newly exposed
for shots of the fast-receding tides,
while the other animals headed for
the highest tops of the trees inland
before floodwaters hit their shores.

The Willow People

*"Cannibalism is moral
in a cannibal country."*
—Samuel Butler

Weeping on the shore
for a mortal humanity,
the willows represent
their old fixed eternity:
since, at any moment,
someone else will die,
they live in mourning
each day of their lives.

But, make no mistake,
this is their permanent
cannibal encampment,
the tribal commitment
to survival, depending
on their daily beatings
of victims, each being
prepared for its eating.

Notes on a Post-Colonial Strongman

"Morality is contraband in war." —Gandhi

1. A Dangerous Dog

Captured somewhere on camera, he stands in
the bush with understandable wariness,
reaching out to address his poor country's poor
who have so long been specifically ignored.

No longer defined by them as figurehead,
falling from himself while falling for himself,
he settles the questions of his people's risks
when unable to peacefully coexist.

Each day is alike as these pictures of him
putting out some new burning spot on the maps
he makes of the skins of his enemies, ones
he has hand-picked for new humiliations.

2. Dog Eat Dog Days

He who's always gotten away with so much
from unrelated knots of 'relatives' now eats
by himself, but doesn't mind preparing them
for his own unpalatable public feasts.

No one is approved unless they choose to go
through the long process of getting through his doors:
since he's the strongest, do they wonder that
his dogs will kill them unless they go on all fours?

He never thought he would fall asleep so soon
after taking them in to be raped in the games
he often plays out. Much later, he'll be seen
staring back from the other side of a screen.

3. Under Surveillance

Should he apologize for lusts as a man,
the lusts that live on into manhood intact?
"If you're not ashamed of what you are doing,"
he asks, "what's the point in even doing it?"

Or, not to attempt what he's done, and will do,
as he looks down and back, should he be rueful
with pity for the child that he was, the man
who, though prosperous, feels slighted nonetheless?

He no longer feels any guilt, none, as far
as we can see, about long-estranged feelings,
since he knows no area in which his powers
aren't extended, enjoying his winnings.

4. Our Serenity

Throughout this, our Selene has kept oddly calm,
not just weeping about all those other men
when we search out the mappings of the fresh lines
wherever they've been drawn upon her by them.

It's hard to tell, through time's telephoto lens,
when she first carelessly raised diffident eyes,
falling beyond sorrows about tomorrows
as she reached down to touch the scars she showed us.

In between, in another smothering game,
new questions arise: Where is that wet pillow
on which 'Turnabout is fair play' had been stitched?
Perhaps she's been taking too much of our drugs?

5. Dream at Year's End

It's tomorrow, or in some earlier time,
in a parish where the villagers were found
to be unfaithful, untruthful, with no one
any longer worth more than his weight in gold.

Then, the picture slowly resolves itself to
an idea of a church, a place where the priest,
prestidigitator of his trade, engaged
in darker crafts, digs up all the victims' graves.

And there the white bones cling like decorations
to that architectural structure obscured
by what seem to be vines of hair covering
skins on the walls of interrogation rooms…

6. Another Year

From a long four seasons confronting wars,
leveled by deaths on this undeveloped river
with its unknown cataracts, this '*long water*'
runs free with contraband, with blood, after.

Revealing how he'd be awkwardly revealed
with his gripping handshakes, unconcealed,
he's just another, corrupt, American puppet
running this country as his personal subject.

If none there loves him, they don't like him
very much. Different, yet with similar skins,
their blood's just the primer for another plot
in which he can never stop it or make it clot.

After 'Kanada'

Months later, warily recovering
from witnessing, beyond any hope
of sorting out who did what to whom,
how he had gone on living as one
already dead, he could still pass
no judgment on how he'd survived,
being taken to a whole new level
of ambiguous understandings
beyond the liberation of the camp.

Now, as he recovers everything
he'd hated, threatening again
to overwhelm, it no longer scares him
as when guards held a gun to his head,
voices still attacking him at rest
in his hospital bed as he stares
out into darkness, as self-contained
as some dictator-for-life– but one
slowly dying of cancers from birth.

Torn between emblems as the doctors
pass by, he wonders if the killing
images can be made less explicit
before he feels too worn down again:
after weeks of breaking rocks he'd lose
his mind if he let them go on working
on him, forced at tongue- or gun-point
until he grew more ready to face
the frank terrors of those one-way trips.

*

This new world is fading into sober
betrayals of his own betrayals,
killing all hints of former glories
as when he played god over the lives
and deaths of others in that place
where cruelty was the main industry.
How could that state, made impossible
for everyone in it, ever survive?
Maybe, he thinks, they're waiting for him

down below, where no ideas or air
would ever flow– yet proofs of one's acts
of complicity might still unfold:
once proud, despite the smells of people
dying like animals, passing through
those mountains of chosen bodies met
beyond the gates– the folded corpses'
flesh spilling into flames– he's burning
everything that fell into his hands…

So, when doctors begin taking down
all his excuses, according to
his once-ruling conviction, to live,
he still can't say what he was doing,
and no longer knows how to go on
signifying what he saw, his mind
overthrown by some final decline
from its own designs, still ticking
inside him like an unexploded bomb.

From The Cultural Revolution

*"Many of them were good
at what they'd been made
to do, making themselves
some heaven of their hell."*

Running through a narrow street
and shouting, 'We want freedom,'
she continued to believe it better
to reach beyond her old teachers.

They said, "Now tell us all about
what things you're running from,
so we know what to do with you
in the new place you're going to."

She had decided when sent away
never to forget– trying, tirelessly,
to fly to that old source of power,
circling like a satellite, for hours.

Was this just inertia carrying her
beyond her expected trajectories,
looking past new, false identities
where she'd continue to be used?

Since she was first 'collectivized,'
she'd suffered, yet still rendered
an homage to the physical world,
as new tenderness came over her:

she got carried away in her work,
with daily diversions, committed
to creating some new bucolic life
from honest trade, a peasant self,

coming to appreciate all the poor
and broken things, knowing how
it could take as many generations
to make that world as good again.

From that damaged future, where
she'd settled, falling back to earth,
crawling across the exhausted soil
in new, urgent, self-examinations,

she yearned to embrace that place
where truths and falsehoods meet,
equaling all of her failure to keep
believing in old, remote, illusions.

She'd proclaim how she changed
to all the skeptics who'd remained
the same. Then, when all was said
and done, she'd be in prison again.

The Current Situation

"For what are stars but asterisks
To point a human life?"
—Emily Dickinson

It's the evening of the seventh day
of a brave new world where shows
of greater tragic possibilities return
every night at right about this time:
it's the Comedy of the Millennium,

a great deal of deaf- and dumbness
threatening, in hilarious ignorance,
to be oblivious; or, just as obvious,
audaciously suspiciously righteous,
giving any new moves a bad name.

Can we make some plan to save us
from the fixers of our Government,
or take new risks about our futures
if they caught us calling right turns
lefts at Assault and Battery Streets?

Could we rise before that audience
to proclaim their bad performance?
What can we do before their public
disclosures of Nothing, spelled out,
but make our plea bargains as well?

Their offer can cost us a great deal,
but unless we get in bed with them
to work out new contracts together,
we might find ourselves threatened,
like beat-up cars waiting to be sold.

After the trial, we might go around
calling ourselves Kings of the Jews.
Wouldn't we be expected to expect
nothing less when facing such stars
with the same fates as ours on earth?

America, 2004

"Can bloody bowls, cups running over
with what eats our guts get any fuller?"

It must have felt like this in Hitler's time:
the swastikas, the ribbons on the cars,
"Support Our Troops," all while we're killing them;
the faith in hate; undemocratic fears
of liberty for all– dead under god–
where silence falls when danger first appears.

While voting blocs only seem spontaneous,
mobs carefully controlled to hold tight sway,
our violent news shows tamp down tragedies
to no unwholesome body parts displayed;
in politics, dark plots excused, released
from new dimensions of horrors every day.

We might conceive of almost anything,
so vast, so fat, and yet so incoherent–
so build our special camps, imprisoning
what represents our future in disgrace:
with little left inside, we'll save our breaths,
declining like another fallen race.

Song for a New Dark Age

King George continues to preside
over the sorry states of things:
no global warming in his eyes,
acids raining down on former greens,
he's giving away state property,
stealing from the coming century.

His agenda still seems popular:
ravishing America's bounty,
feeding fears, promoting wars
in return for seeding scenery
with money plants, shaping a nation
to fit its childlike population.

Like greedy children now, we turn
our savings into shopping lists,
ignoring atmospheric terms
that run from rising tides to risks
of changing radiance on earth
promoting cancers, shining death–

some final little ornaments
to adorn his and the future face
of famine, for all governments
to join his club, the New Dark Age.

A Dream of New Orleans

Since a perfect storm's expected churning up
of what had been before, not giving up
on fighting chaos, you still don't know why
some houses stay afloat upon those tides.

Nor is it easy to account for things
like musical resistance, jazz still playing
in islets, dry havens nearby– and yet,
committed to reversals, that's the best

you can do: wet, molting like butterflies
in final stages of metamorphoses,
when all the feeling begins flooding back,
along with other death-defying acts...

When some sommelier, moments earlier,
was lying out along a drowning pier,
still floating underwater, covered by
barrels of slick black tar in the night,

you went to grab his hands to that music
and danced him back to the shore, ironic
as you worked up to his level, his eyes.
But, as the music plays on, he says,

"For us to ever even these scores
and return to what was rightfully ours,
must we take up slaughtering figures
of inundation, forget who we were?"

The hardest part will be clearing this mess,
the bloated bodies blooming in darkness,
more dangerous waiting, increasing harm.
For safety's sake, you fold him in your arms.

State Politician Arriving Late

New Orleans, 2005

An undisciplined dog at an end
of his tether, he asks so little of
himself that he can hardly bark
Fuck you hard enough, or think
how many must have died; but,
while he tries to cover his back,
it's not so easy to seem relaxed.

To ease his conscience perhaps,
he will leave no residual marks,
as gruesome as his government
papering over certain evidence:
survivors hanging off the roofs,
starving to edges of extinctions
those its rations can easily feed.

Will pincers on a people seized
say enough of just how corrupt
the choice was to give them up?
When drowning, nothing is left
but to help himself, let them hit
concrete, inspiring in him more
whining, a plea for his reprieve.

Transitory Creatures

As a part of America sinks
into its own smug stupidity,
what's a democracy to me?
Newspapers, full of photos,
political positions in which
one understands that a bust
of someone, living or dead,
signifies nothing more than
what has already been said
about energy independence.

Journalists, if I begged you
to stand up, would you just
put all those stories to rest?
As we'd decimate the skies,
clouds under which we'd try
to puzzle out what was true
about the myth of a Mother
who'd live for her Children
but married a younger Man
who started ravishing them,

as boots slam the pavement,
hands asleep in my pockets
dream of a peace: *I've seen
quite enough of what we'll
see quite enough of,* I think.
On this island, we float free
all day, sink to the bottoms
at night, covered with gold-
colored liquids, viscous oils
eclipsing the shivering skin.

In Stunned Silence

The electoral process won't work
this time around against terrorists
when 'no man is an island' is trumped
by confusions of faith. We'll stop this

cunning churning, the wizened chisels
in our hands and heads, when we may
no longer hear ourselves think, and say,
What is this lull inside of my thoughts?

We think we could've been warned that
this is the real world, but we can't tell
if it's pointing towards an end to all
our wars, or the end of something else.

Or is it just a monument to
building momentum, the advent of
a bloody kiss for everyone who
is living in this time and place

where we're all already occupied
in bringing down yet another race?

"A Somber Obama..."

—New York Times headline

New news of the wars comes to us
with counts of soldiers' deaths; of course,
he'd rather not seem symptom or cause.

Full of debts from social contracts,
with politics as usual,
now he's televising the "facts,"

showing us what he's going through
to find some way to return to
a state sustaining meaning and sense.

He'd plumb our depths, but it appears
we're all backed up, huge white underwear
strewn everywhere, like flags of surrender.

Till we know how he does it, and why,
he's swimming underwater in
a deep cup of clear and bright blue sky.

From the Inland Sea

It was a time of brilliant whimsy,
when we didn't feel like anything
but inclined to talk and talk, or play.

It was our social philosophy
that we found by the same inland sea
as some old overturned policies–

still thinking we were a part of this
experiment's metamorphosis
of experience– as if we'd gone

window-shopping for a prediction
of an end to all the policies
that began in 1933…

It was a democratic process
that seemed new as vivid white semen
staining the darker sky we'd chosen

to live beneath; and then, in-between,
if we weren't feeling too beaten
down about our anger for a change,

driven to find something deeper then,
we would patiently wait for the end.

II.
Reports from Babylon

"There is a crack, a crack in everything–
that's how the light gets in."
—Leonard Cohen

Mission to the Gentiles

At first we were famished with thirst
along those arid, acrid-scented ways,
which were long, uphill, rising away
from darker corners of their universe.

With their fallen fruit on either hand,
while we were prepared, taking care
not to be taken in by their brazen air
for our extended sojourn in that land,

what we saw there, within our terms,
within those souls, we couldn't deny:
it became our primary roles, to apply
some rules to those chaotic concerns.

Where lately we passed, unsurprised
that a chastisement of circumstances
extended beyond old dervish dances
to their residues of sacrifice besides,

after a time our continuing the climb
found us closer, but made less sense
within that greater loss of innocence:
not blinded by distance or overcome,

we saw all their resistance to change
as straining to retain a life unopened
by what we brought of hope to them,
until we reached the end of our days.

Revolutionary Recruits

"Many were infected by the poison,
babies burned, bankers shot dead:
matter didn't fault this destruction."

They have big dreams, the same as us,
but much more cynical honesty about
how killing is the best political policy.

Karma-makers, schooled by violence,
they began with their bold obedience,
without moral sense, to murdering us.

As parasites evolved, to feed on them,
new weapons would effectively clean
the world of all those necessary dead:

they even sacrifice themselves to take
an undetectable bomb onto the planes,
and once they destroy the cities' walls,

or when we're released into the hands
of their zealous public thought-police,
they needn't attack those places again.

Their sickle moon casts long shadows
across our world, covering everything.
Yet, blowing up old political systems,

ending with settings up of themselves,
they still might find similar symptoms:
flying high, what skies will *they* scan?

Advent of Another War

Here's a piece of property
we're going to go through
to kill all the wild animals
because of this oil-stained
plunder from years before.

This is the violent heritage
of a province where blood
drowns a whole landscape,
as we, who'd sacrificed all
that desert wildlife, would.

Hanging above in drier air,
this wish lives at the limits
of our luck, the prayer that
can be more fully engaged
by a new proof of our rage.

Now, we say, and put them
all to sleep as if war is just
elaborate dream dictations,
waging death till its names
no longer solve a problem.

Fists raised to that iron sky,
sickly-hued, God-humbled,
holding the gun at our side,
we'll weep, without shame,
at the ends of sports events,

pushing past the goalposts,
breaking through to an end
of the field, gathering coins
with no future dates shining
from the depths of dry wells.

Photographer Embedded in Old World Orders

He's being watched, shooting what he's seen
within the rings of walls, the guarded temples,
peripheral among these stricken peoples
who'll soon become "Iraqi citizens."

He charts each change as 'democracy' spreads,
where ruined walls of mud around them make
each face seem harder than that broken brick–
though surely some of them will soon be dead.

Conflicted, he knows what they've got to lose,
how choices come to fall on fighting men
who'll learn that "peace" may guarantee no end
to corpses, who've let themselves be used,

and realize how much bitterness endures
as a consequence of others' policies,
luxuries distributed unequally
creating fires from silenced engines' roars.

So what will he shoot, how does he even choose?
This forced forgetfulness of self's a test
he can't complete– to conquer, or accept
the harder lesson: "If not your life, then whose?"

He sleeps inside his clothes on floors of vans
alongside roads where bodies rot, and knows
that soon, behind stone walls, he too must go
the same hard way that yields more smoking guns.

Yet, he'll still stop before each bloody aftermath:
Why should one crow take up the whole birdbath?

Soldier Hiding in a Clearing

With so many busy beggars near at hand
standing up to your life in the safe haven,
building new anti-government coalitions
of the proudly poor or violently ignorant,
it's impossible now for you to ever verify
whose bombs may tear your world apart;
but, at any rate, soon nothing will be left.

You hear the sound of terror everywhere,
surpassing its commencement, going out,
but your eyes are turned, beyond revision
of the meanings to be read into a passage
through the burning tissues of these days:
all you see is dramatic irony in a betrayal
of enemies *versus* being betrayed by fate.

Because you wished to please that leader
out not only for your head but your heart,
hearing the earnest egocentric arguments,
accepting that language beyond insincere,
you receive the received opinions unseen
in the sun, self-containment broken open
as nuances seem more than you can bear.

Communicating what none wants to hear,
that God's will can't be made any clearer
and a death for a god won't be any easier,
fire-breathing about outcomes paying off
in embroidered fabrics, surrendered flags,
what once seemed truths about tomorrow
become just carnage, beyond camouflage.

Questions in Iraq

We depend on this light,
we say, to aid our sight,
putting ourselves inside
our big columns of it as
it takes us in or enemies
throw us back. But now,
as we sort ourselves out,
we feel pensive, passive,
asking which ways to go.

We don't mind being one
of these many in a mass,
weaning ourselves from
talking about the rest of
those others still begging
the camp commander for
some information about
everything they've done,
everything lying strewn.

So many hard questions
of old ghostly presences:
we experience increases
in stimulus and motives
in the old crockery shop
where clay pages began,
made by the people who
started out by assuming
no Laws, and no peace.

And now, they still offer
little more for our praise
than blurred inscriptions
bleeding through the days.

A Foreign Correspondent

Speaking from fronts, not giving up
on divulging some new information
from your investigation of the facts
others give their own political spins,

you give us your alternative version
and hold interviews with politicians
all out of control, holding their own
dirt-bag dialogues with their worlds.

While they dance their public dance,
we begin to see things for ourselves:
the ways one finds oneself in power,

answering threats, creating seamless
narratives from a White House lawn
to cemeteries full of new Iraqi dead.

Debriefing

"Take these remarks, for what they're worth,"
he says: "For many years, departing officials
were expected not to question their concerns
about our principles on this tight little island.

You think we keep reading these documents
because we don't want to miss out on things,
not even the formulaic critique that someday,
you think, may win you the medal you covet."

There are two different kinds of horror there,
internal and *external*, its boring bureaucracy
that must be saved in some forms to whisper
inexact answers to governing policy-makers.

He wishes us what we can only dream about:
that we'll go away, with nothing more to say.

Repatriation

"We're each our own unreliable witness,
whose yield from the vanishing world is
our feeling like smuggled-out antiquities."

Abroad so long with what you always feared,
that you might never be allowed to stay,
now, yards away from what you once desired,
you bow beneath some politicians' sway.

With books of bureaucratic interests, plans
and edicts signed and posted on the doors,
a country holds its strength from strangers' hands–
and soon you'll know what you must answer for.

Left to yourselves, you read the secret signs;
on creeping feet, you must accept this day
this loss of trust. "The body's not designed
to be impervious to this world," they say.

Intruding on terrain where you'll return
to what your futures may be meaning to hold,
it seems to smell of ash, like something burned–
its undisputed logic, beyond you, cold.

Theater of War

It's been a long war, as you can attest:
the generals said that you were so brave,
but you only did what *they* told you to,
   Suck it up, instead of falling apart.

You knew yourselves in terms of such success,
but not through designs or lines you made up,
portraying different soldiers on that stage
   with different degrees of verisimilitude…

If scars are written now across each face,
time will show you what happens when you fail–
as when, back home, you're left with the meanings
your words can't describe, still missing inside
   what's become of all the action you knew:
   now and forever, "missing in action."

Ghost after Torture

Are you the one who felt
so dominant, whose life
contained a regiment,
who slaughtered a mother
who taught her children
not so well how to live?

Now that you've shown us
lost innocence, you don't
need more money to fall
back on another war:
you are where you were,
and make your images

terribly physical,
suitably mystical,
so you can still do what
you think a man alone
should render for himself,
his fate alive within.

Banquet

It was a cornucopia
of lies you lived on for years,
and it sustained you awhile

with its bitter back story
and news bites upon the hides
of others as you agreed

to maintain imperturbability
throughout the many hours
of your mutual needs.

At the end of all this,
some of us still trusted love:
it would be just one week

before other family men
went home, but at your own
wedding banquet you just sat

still there, unable to eat.

Operations

If old war injuries will lead
to new operations, if 'Good
replacement parts may cost
an arm or a leg' as they say,
it's more bad news, for you:
you'll have to stay this way.

You, who wanted that mess
of sutures, tapestries in skin,
to return you to better repair,
squander your time in jokes
that no one else could guess
what your scars really cloak.

Odd, how one's body yields
to the soul, as when the new
takes the old: no longer you
at the controls, yet your turn
to choose, all this difference
lies in that distance between

the doctors who'd help fight
mortality for you… and you,
who still resist your chances
to shed a light or even speak
of bodies, wrapped in sheets,
while your bedsprings creak.

As you're going under again,
the raft of the familiar slides
over all your mercurial tides,
setting forth those old bones
still breaking, in a new wave
of pain, piling up like stones.

Report from Babylon

"Stiff necks are necks in nooses."

They send up new burnt offerings
to keep the bonds of their old pacts
with constant death and destruction
in Babylon, in light of these facts:

those subject to other gods' regimes
must suffer, die young– by torture,
starvation, bombings by children–
and everyone dies, sooner or later…

When I think of winners and losers
among the gods, I just have to laugh–
for what, in all their old testaments,
separates the wheat from the chaff?

The Law's like falling off the wagon:
first, the act; then, guilty repentance;
rules passed on sins by other sinners;
then, finally, the harshest sentence.

Nothing's forgotten, nor forgiven,
in endless cycles of justice, blind
to all those quivering politicians
held in the hands of their own kind:

always, the same investigations,
after which an underling is hanged;
then comes their own exonerations–
and the cycles begin all over again.

III.
National Pastimes

That baseball that you throw
at ninety miles an hour today
may be another hit tomorrow.

Bitter Pills

If you have the patience
to work toward a goal,
stick to what you started,

and then, to maintain
the desire to prosper,
giving yourself over

to continuing to deal
with old worn-out wants
while defining others

by their different kinds
of commitments, what
will typically happen

is that those bitter pills
will be taken by mouth,
by the glass, with great

difficulty, until you sort
things out and swallow
them all down, eagerly.

On the Job

*"I don't know why we're here, but I'm sure
that it's not in order to enjoy ourselves."*
—Ludwig Wittgenstein

It was all about our piecework in the dark,
and commonplace cowardice, functioning
in the face of how we ached against fears
of accommodating to resentment and rage

against insecurity, hemmed in, turning on
ourselves, never questioning our situation,
our deference in our own panting defense;
deflecting, if we only waited long enough,

how it wasn't helpful for us to stay stoned
to get through the weeks with all the other
workers getting high– and, because it was
useful for our managers to keep us in line,

they'd carefully delineate, out in the open,
our commodious needs, to stay at our jobs.

Workers with Nowhere Else to Go

When, near the end, we struggled to see
exactly where we were in our lives
without adjectives, with completely
different views about our former selves,

our bosses warned us, intent upon
destined usurpers for our lowly roles,
making molehills out of our mountains
by digging ourselves into new holes:

whole new catalogs of how we were
slowed by work-related injuries,
over-extended, going nowhere,
or where they thought we ought not to be,

delineating to infinity how
we all should have been replaced by now.

Fighting Fires with Fire

1.

They called the troops together to resolve
how they'd call us together, putting us in
a position where we'd be left on our own,
trying to light some fire among ourselves.

Sometimes there were just enough 'fixed'
applications for the job; so, in those days,
we set our goal, waited till they called us,
and weren't surprised by the simple facts,

counting on veterans to fill us in on them:
we were the last ones taken, always were
resented, and yet we never knew for sure
who abused our use of this 'second home'

where everyone seemed about to be fired.
Beyond barriers, which stumped us anew,
we trained until they'd deliver their news:
because everything was about those fires,

we'd kept up, with burning determination
to enforce our new truces, when we went
out, zealously trying to discover how best
to save ourselves from a burning building.

2.

With our lives full of vibrations from fire alarms,
with them all going off at one and the same time,
past those slicked poles we'd come sliding down,
we waited through heavy footsteps of long hours
for some calls to come in, new burnings to begin.

They said, "There aren't any pussies around here
to serve or save you just because you feel hungry,
burning to be a man, or woman," until we'd seen
our lives in a whole new light, ones passed down
from those uniformed fathers to their lowly sons.

Still learning from our instruction manuals about
how to turn on new systems, yet coming to terms
with the hydraulic hoses malfunctioning, beyond
those barriers, we still weren't happy about being
compliant or complicit with what we'd had to do.

We were trading tirades on the ruining of houses,
staring at the footage of their systematic lootings,
even as we drew our sad, new conclusions about
that deference to our superiors, who often yelled,
"You've been answering too many false alarms!"

3.

With nothing left to look at but survivors
facing burns, waving white flags, as once
we'd thought the saving of people's lives
was a good way to get some pictures into
the papers, those compendiums of 'heroic'
or typical tasks, and all starring ourselves,

we'd carried them out to tentative havens,
getting wet as when we tried to save them
from the greater pressures from the hoses,
diving into those streams of water, falling
through those gradients with what powers
we had, finding only shells of their rooms.

Brooding about all the houses we let burn,
we came back at night with our flashlights
to reopen the cases, to find out: if only we
had reached out, blown smoke away from
the staircase, or broken open that window,
would that have made any real difference?

Where were our disinterested logic's flaws
then? Returning to tamp down the embers,
still alive, waiting for these fires to die out,
were we supposed to feel bad, as we knew
we'd be feeling, all that immense intensity,
intense immensity, for the rest of our lives?

Small Town Cop

A young officer takes an oath
of office, settling down to say
he's not lazy, like those others
that he saw lying down across
the street, closing pearly gates
for small town boys gone bad.

Never forgetting this and how
police officers must cooperate
with authorities when they put
their family's lives on the line,
for once, his "life" is revealed;
or is he just too slow to know?

With lips pressed to his badge,
against each other, closing up,
he'd press each case to its end,
this withheld white guy's kind
of god. But, how will he know
when his gun becomes a cross,

and, folded inside the uniform,
known to him as boy and man,
how, finally, will he be found?

Iconographies of Money

The young reporter of the financial scene
would visit houses he never could afford,
relying on inside invitations to do his job.

But new-moneyed interests did their jobs
on him: in urgent self-expressions, falling
back to earth, they were all seen crawling

on the stock exchange's floors, accepting
futures with an embrace of iconographies
in which a life equals the need to hold on

to wealth's remote illusion, the unbroken
chain of fences that encircled The Bourse
until overrun by the people of Paris, once.

Manqué in a Cage

When this busy business person feels
harried beyond his powers of speech,
he opens his dustier vaults and keeps
to undersides of tiers of ledger books
resting inside a calm collective quiet,
not quite ready yet to give this all up;
yet, getting and spending, he reflects
how he has pressed all possible flesh.

He can guess into what spectral form
his flesh will decline, but peering out
from a darkened window at the other
restless workers, he decides he might
be seen, if only by the losers, who do
their work just to give it up, and want
to leave no immortal name, unable to
forget this life inside this glass house.

Sweating as if taking tests depending
only on his lousy long-term memory,
prisoner of inconstant constituencies,
he passes through steel doors, sounds
alarms; yet, thinking he might get by
on pride, he takes a moment to resist:
'If now it feels as if I've fallen down,'
he says, 'I must have risen up before.'

The Player

Sputtering within their wintry clothes,
cold bodies jolted by ambivalent bolts,

it doesn't take weeks, however soiled
with mud colors, melting into a world,

for people to show their sharper teeth–
but he always plays someone who sees

how a player gallops ahead of the pack
or starts a car engine with just a spark,

while still protesting, loudly, and long,
how cowardice consists of never trying.

Walls become his foils and, as they fall,
he no longer allows his victims to tell,

through all their tortures and mayhem,
masters from monsters who play them.

A Saint

Her life was sad because
since she was very young
she yearned to be a saint,

and when she got older,
got married, had two sons,
she still loved all the pain

from such self-sacrifice—
but didn't have a chance
to become sanctified

until after she'd died,
when her first-born son,
Richard Nixon, resigned:

he said she was a saint,
and even cried a little,
pausing in the middle

of his resignation
that played on national
network television.

'Friends of Bill'

1.

He's a dynamo in person, electromagnetic
wherever he goes, fast along his own path
of least resistance; as, now, he only hopes
to appear, with such allures still upon him,
as beautifully smoothing through his days.

He chews over surfaces, like wood-boring
insects, intractable facts: it's as if all these
buzzing beings, their spontaneous swarms,
are an appropriate trope for shining clouds
of feelings, flying onto, and into, our skins.

So he's fanning us with his thicker breeze,
which leads to some other hazes he leaves,
that leads to his distanced eyes, full of lies
about how he wants to assert his 'authority.'
If his best hope for some quick escape lies

in rearranging words, performing on stage,
this theatricality becoming restless enough
for him to act out in more dangerous ways,
he's still afraid of looming thunder-clouds,
and sleeps in darkened rooms, just in case.

2.

As a morning norm he's fallen into,
he's doing his squats in sweatpants,
condescending, as if there still were
an old blaze in his complacent gaze.
Soon he may have to trust just what
we had to do to keep him out of jail.

Any old loyalty becomes a problem
if we don't know how he would use
the killing word, or spill out figures,
walking a fine line into a bar where
we hang out, composing each night,
until we figure something better out.

Comparing wiping conscience away
during our dinner talks of such stuff,
he doesn't take our bait for a debate;
but, missing his good old arguments,
it boils down to the last time his life
was a matter of nightly recognitions.

Now, rather than plan that far ahead,
it's a great strain to see in his sprays
of showers, flowers. He was the god
whose eyes played such tricks on us;
all language was, especially for him,
just a thing a spin doctor would spin.

Some More Bad Ideas

*"In politics, absurdity
is not a handicap."*
—Napoleon Bonaparte

Right off, he tells us how
he's had hard work to do,
but this has so little to do
with clearing underbrush
or the mending of fences.

An acting politician who
seems comforting knows
how it secures him votes
to show us how he holds
a hammer, its sharp claw

for pulling out of the law;
yet, some people believe
in what he's giving them
to trust in, seeing heaven
or hell, all by themselves.

Immigration Official

He dreams portraits of dark heads,
and the masses of hair fine-etched
in black lines down backs become
the focus in the frames within one
big picture that seems like his little
window into a much greater world.

Where many more dark women sit
within some other tropical gardens,
he peers beyond those lush flowers
through windows, a shifting vision
revealing other darker parts within
those private dreamy observations.

He never sees their painting whole:
of the many things he wishes them
to do, he knows they may never go
where he wants them to, as, before
they'd even arrive, those who tried
escaping their countries often died.

When those dreams were still fresh
he weaved his macroscopic scenes,
but it's like a skin graft or pastiche,
hard to fit each new piece to while
he scrupulously decides what fates
he would make for their short lives.

At the cost of some loss, of dignity,
he finds himself re-enrolling, then,
in that program for *illegals* issuing
forth onto hot sidewalks in droves,
searching for and reaching toward
their unreachable too distant goals.

Will he abandon all his sentencing,
finding that they're not even guilty,
or is this just another bad example
of an 'open door policy' made long
before his time? Ending his dream,
he cries, *Let my eyes be open*, then.

Intelligence Agency

1.

They rise as the sun rises, casting long shadows
across the land. Reentering the outstretched palms
of this world, they're still, trying to interpret how,
as a matter of course, soft noises masked by crowds,
so few of those who hear their voices would accept
their timelier warnings. Returning to their house,

they want to spill together into some reservoir
where water will be warm– but they've been warned before:
pausing from gazing out to sea, then back to shore,
they've witnessed births of unexpected torrents there
under mirroring skies reflecting in the clouds
a beach beneath a shroud descending more and more.

It seems that now they're standing on opposing sides
of deeper currents, with a new relationship
between the waves rippling toward them like rapids while,
decreasing, virtual light flows beyond their sight.
Do they think they can take their places on this map?
"You'll come to me, blowing like those winds," she smiles.

Missing engagements with their respective critiques,
they'd advocate the best within their natures' range,
a great weight lifting heavenward for them to speak:
"Are we inside this world for all the world to see
how we carry deep divisions of pain, unchanged?"
"An empty sack, an always-driven wind, that's me..."

2.

Old social events recorded between their lips,
following slick routes to the interior,
they both desire, beyond these temporary trips,
their own words to escape others' ideas of them–
reading documents without approval, a complex
of shadows beyond which they may see only blame.

With the long-lost alphabets of some old dreams
washing over them as they would wash raw meat
in preparation for some upcoming feast,
reading leaves to bring the words of others closer
to their own, they think: "If we could only recognize
their strictures, it might put us in the picture."

They've been pasting papers into papier-maché,
reaching back to childhood's even breathing in and out,
such predilections betraying their time and place:
listening for some shyer notes made bold to go
beyond their words, avoiding harder obstacles,
they'd ride out where toll roads no longer take their tolls.

They feel confused, but reconfirmed by being
confined to the jobs they know they have to do:
isn't it reasonable, gradually seeing
others' mistaken takes on their free-wheeling breaths,
always yearning to return to themselves again,
to want reversals of birth, incompetence, death?

Once, they thought, "We can't eat while anyone starves,"
just wanting to live a more exemplary life–
but what good did their never eating ever serve?
They wish they could patch things up, yet still remember
finding themselves embittered with everyone else
living out their own traumatic family dramas:

"Those people you want to be reunited with
are dangerous, being so close to being you."
And so, they'd average out their material gifts,
feeling increasingly inconsequential, sure
that they'd lose all their memories of the poetry
of a past no one else seems to want anymore.

After they've come to some hard-won conclusions
about their situation, difficult new terms
superseding readings of them by anyone,
they want to make all of those others understand
that they've still been faithful, though feeling forsaken,
lost in engagements with the physical land.

Knowing all the tools of their trade wouldn't affect
the holes growing cruder and deeper around them,
without authority, which others would reject,
if nothing else, no one else is prone to explore
that old democracy ruling under the ground–
yet, going out, they think, they might soon be no more.

4.

Earth recovers their flesh, oblivious, obscured,
forever masking its healing by leaving
all their problematic occasions unexplored;
though they wouldn't complain, often even have fun,
like other agents, they know they'll hardly get by
with thinking that someday they both might be broken.

Still fearing how revolving stars set up new traps
with their preternatural determinations,
they cycle in circles; after many long laps,
wheels rolling beneath them with manic energy,
although the leather seats and metal frames are hard
between their legs, they feel they're sitting prettily.

Soon enough, they go rolling into freshened air,
out beyond the stresses that, day by day by day,
some bright night voices wake them to, in their glare.
The best parts are when they can fit in some fitful
images past all private harms– what a couple
of beasts, being together at least, might still fulfill.

At home, she says, "this is the place we are because
it seems the right size for us to be." He answers,
"No one else can make a case for what someone does;
it's often the best way for the work to get done–
but now it's up to orthodox others to find
their own congenial, unorthodox solutions."

5.

Though it doesn't warp them to hold to each other,
they think they can actually take hold only
when others leave them alone beyond a closed door…
But, before they can say "I do," they agree to be
tested at the behest of those offices where
passports and licenses are stamped for a fee.

"Let's put on some sort of universal gas masks,"
they joke, "so we won't have to die from our own fumes
before our damned personas start blowing apart,"
indebted to this notion– although there are times
they see themselves float among picnic baskets past
their natural inclinations to just get by.

With ants crawling over them, betraying some pains
medications couldn't quell, soon they're becoming
cozily domestic, returning home again
to indulge themselves in such benevolence
from first to last, remaining on some honeymoon
in spite of those nights spent together in silence.

"We may grab someone, keep them with us to survive,
but is it as good as being by ourselves
in a desert somewhere, like the last of our tribe?"
Then, getting further away, surviving long drought
in a new warming trend: "Since this old job has been
so hard on us, let's try to carve our own way out."

6.

All the old pictures becoming more explicit,
their dealings in time seem as formal as people's
from previous generations: the jobs they quit,
putting those bewilderments behind them, the noise–
then, drafting behind, drifting by in their car,
with voices still positive and none the less poised.

They've rejected the public styles of those whose looks
tied their hands, as privately they joke about
those who read all their lives through library books,
official bulletins, on their paperbacked shelves,
odd works filed under different numbers and names:
"They'll have to figure some things out for themselves..."

Years later, they've been posted by their government
to a happier place. Newly arrived, their bodies
weigh about the same, the way they are by then.
As the lopped trees begin, by the ends of these days,
to send up new shoots, they are where they wished to be,
not languishing till some final offer is made.

Their house in the forest, in which they live alone–
old mold remaining in the wood, rising, aflame,
asserted itself through smoke, positively shone.
And never again will there be, they think, even cloned,
two others with their unique personalities,
particular histories, after they are gone.

IV.
Captive Celebrations

"The only thing that stands between greatness and myself is me."
—Woody Allen

Voices of the Imminent Dead

"Do you feel lost, without a cause,
now that you're the wingèd ones?"

1.

From opposite sides of the streets, we hear
their attitudes expressed: Whosoever sheds
the blood of anyone, except in self-defense
from bodily harm, will never go to heaven.

With every voice contested, compromised,
as murderers seize power, arming for wars,
soon our only hope will be to be left alone,
with our talents and labor no longer secure.

Days pass and many more become shut up,
cut off at their roots, playing out new roles,
some living for their sad attempts at coups
against these killers, disobeying their rules.

They'd write their letters in narrow spaces,
behind barred windows, yet unvanquished
though being beaten by vicious policemen;
in harder times, the beatings undiminished.

2.

Taken by chariots of fire across their skies,
we study afterlives, returning to that blood
we found in insubstantial shapes, in flames
as in their words, down to their last period.

With so much in common, we've survived
to tell their tales of the passing generations
growing old together, with rising pressures
from the new, living, usurping populations.

Still wishing for a peace we've never seen,
friends restored past banishment or doubts;
those idealized forms in unvarnished terms
are what we inevitably cannot speak aloud.

3.

For us to make the sacrifice, to try to begin
our lives all over again, are we able to sing
out new narratives when worrisome omens
suggest that we disengage from everything?

We live alone with our heavy consciences,
nights closing in on us, covering our heads
with these images, so everyone who is sick
with forgetting may live in similar distress.

We sleep poorly now, because we sold out
for greasing squeaky wheels, while scenes
of conflicts provoke us now to shout about
these conditions, living in the dying dream:

when, in unguarded moments, we mention
disaster-driven losses, of faces unforgotten,
remaining in shadows– then, and only then,
do we hunger, for a change, to be forgiven.

Interim in Sector Gris

"If I'm going to rest, rest assured, I want
no crisis or murderous crossing of what
lies stuck inside of me, no final versions
of those old humiliating shapes of things."

When there came a knocking at our door,
the prayer-seller begging in a whisper for
donations, it raised new ethical questions:
do we send him packing or give him alms?

Since none were asked, none given before,
it made sense to question then: What next?
or What's it all about? Still feeling bound
by a staircase, with the word Cambio on it,

we wondered whether all the intermediate
steps could give some cover until we were
ready for answers to life's larger questions
haunting the house in which we were born.

Homeless Harry Sold His House

He stands beyond your fence and claims to grieve
for those who feel their deepest grievances
are hung like gauze between themselves and him:
"I've come to tell you, not as you suppose,
that there are other ways to find transcendence
from your fallen state; I'll show you the way
you each must start to leave this world, alone.

The factors that control your lives are how
you choose to purchase things you think that you
can't live without. Why shouldn't people question
just why they must exist inside this cage
they're dying in? You carry dreams like leaves
now sliding down drenched streets together
into drains, the body's dark fluids below."

The only one who understands attending
to such mysteries exonerates himself
from blame: "I know all walls must someday fall–
and they will fall on you," he says. Suspicious
still of what might be his plot– a narrative
with some devils in them, or devils not–
now you're standing firm, taking this all in.

Since you don't hold by his simple faith in
either/or– that you'll be saved or else be doomed
by fate to be apostate– he's scuttling off
to where he'll show others how to bow their heads.
Yes, you'll die before believing in his chapter
and verse, the inventions and inversions of
his first, and only, fundamental church.

Around a Barrel Fire

It's gotten late but they don't care
to be doing much of anything, for,
creatures of cold comfort in order,
shrugging off their material goods,
they've become so adept at hiding
their original urgencies to simplify
that they often crash or often burn.

They keep a drunken orbit, traced
around their hidden arrangements
of bodies on the pavement, where
their careers are in constant flight
in loops about their golden glows,
modeling the planets, from below
the moon's phases, filling a space.

Falling down now in falling snow,
by concrete steps, around a corner,
liquefying the life soon to be over,
they can almost taste this future as
they must have veered, once flush,
from pasts with long receding nets
of footprints, down dark corridors.

They wake, seeping up from sleep
the drinks from flasks don't freeze,
their memories of murderous lives
and flesh resented for representing
its excrescences, a deepening dusk
providing, like a new burning fuel,
smoke rising into fading afternoon.

Sleeping in The Mission

In the absence of any heroic scenes,
unnatural lights of this world going out,
now he's carefully cultivating the thought,
'Never again this day.' Then, as in a dream,

'It's an astonishment, which begins at home,'
he thinks, on a toilet seat that's seen its share
of ass-wipes in its time– yet, he barely cares
if they have a whole damned voluntary room

full of homeless down there: he's often slept
on such Christian floors. Sure, it's a hard sell,
but, it's certainly a good warm up– for hell:

having waited long enough for his bad end,
as their symbolism enters his body's house,
he'll flow back to its impenetrable source.

Escaping Childhood

*"Be not too hasty to trust or admire
teachers of morality: they discourse
like angels, but they live like men."*
—Samuel Johnson

1.

We took a lot of flak, but slipped away
from the speeches on the public square
where a people let their liberties erode
in an urgency of made-up emergencies.

Taking in what a crowd brought about,
seeing everyone else was fighting over
pieces of the pie, the problem was war
becoming our own scripted nightmare.

Getting caught in unidentifiable masks
with wild animals' eyes, aging took us
more than miles past their comfortable
limits of murmuring trees, dead leaves.

By then, we were laughing and crying,
in fits, failing to cope with our copious
opportunities to slip through a doorway
with no chances left to re-enter society.

2.

How hard, we remember, those early years,
much too poor for our tastes: unchallenged,
how tall those black hills before us seemed,
some lesser hills not so hard for us to climb.

With everything decaying, or melting away
into clouds, for each speech with an almost
comical a-historical twist, is it too late now
to ask, "Why didn't you warn us?" of them?

Is new self-knowledge only our old designs
to cancel out our names, leaving us without
good accounts left to tell? Will we ever find
exactly what we want from somebody else?

As symbols drained away, we could display
our old arguments within some older terms:
"You may take the deep fears out of the boy,
but they still control a morality-driven man.

3.

If we took these questions back and re-edited
our lives for some more practical information,
would we find all our original answers within
ourselves, these living jungles, by such means?

If they removed our names from the registries
of regicides, is there anything that can stop us
from going through the castle walls, at a pace
no other will may control, at our convenience?

In forced marches past the victorious gestures
of kings and queens, on horses with their guns,
we take no pleasure in being at the crossroads
of great big junk piles of people, in the dumps.

Now we're winded, passing bluffs, with a tug
from tangoing guitars, headed for the far hills,
where wild animals would eat from our hands
until chilling air fills all the holes in our lungs.

Green Dream

A bright sunny day in late spring: a man
walking along long rows of lush flowers
stops to listen for all those green dreams
approaching him down the colorful path.

Warm sun arcing over the park, the man
thinks he's being followed, by a younger
man watching from a bench, or the older
man veering from a path, musing nearby.

Acting under the plot's sway, the actors,
named 'Paul Newsome,' 'Peter Concrete,'
are humming: "*If you won't begin living,
you'll never become a full human being.*"

He hopes he's not lying to himself when
he says, "*I must lose my enemies. I can't
let myself get killed.*" He digs in, staring
at a leaf. Usually, his paranoia looks like

a carved-on walking stick, a calling card,
but now it feels like a gift from strangers,
and, continuing to grow inside his layers,
it seems life's greatest hope for a change.

Apostate Casting Stones

While others start by strewing token stones
along a pilgrims' path, he stands and stares
behind a folding-screen. He waits awhile
in dirt, becoming sick of abject tones
that lead to racing hearts at heightened speech,
those scintillating formal phrases from
before– the gods' forsaken languages
once used to comprehend uncertainties.

Some choose to close their eyes to sing out past
their constant threatening to go in winds'
complex and new directions; yet, content
to know how all their arms could never cast
away old doubts or fears, can he record
his own accomplishments? Someday he may,
who goes away to practice how to stay
alive outside communities of words…

He feels an old disgust with those who vex
those ancient rites, as if the words control
all the corrupt unruly images
that live within their momentary flux,
and thinks rejecting heritage demands
dramatic breaks from pasts: that circumstance,
its future tense, unlike gods' winds, may bear
those up who let their indecision stand.

With speculations now about the choice
of living well beyond his hedonistic
self-concerns, he'd question certain maunderings
regarding what those gods once said, and voice
how what they did or didn't do about
their love for him suggests they knew by heart
just who it was who came to pray, who stepped
outside of what they once themselves begot.

Though they, who say they never said they'd howl
insistently upon their windy heights,
might show him how to still keep still, rolled in
a ball, or, rolling on, till time would tell
what chance is left for him to leave– till then,
as bodies disappear from all their beds,
this information holds each fretful face
abstracted or abashed: like most of them,

who, sleeping late until they're kissed awake,
seem waiting for an old machinery
of words to hold some sway between them, say,
"To crave this world would be a sad mistake,"
with stacks of bloody stones that steam like drafts
of freedom rising from each altar-ed place,
he hopes to save some chance at happiness–
"Please let this cold meat sleep," his epitaph.

Walking California

Rather than submit yourself to the skies
you walked so fast and far away beneath,
refusing soon to stop and find out why
you'd suffer casualties for what you'd need,
you thought at first it wouldn't be so hard
avoiding stays in emergency rooms–
but, raining cats and dogs then, unlike gods,
you found you still had lots of work to do.

You couldn't deny what others had done,
thinking they knew the real person, the man,
with nothing completely neutral as when
you finally took yourself off their hands.
Where you'd been, many who you knew were gone,
some with whom you'd shared a body or mind–
but most, remaining, were just hanging on,
broke, broken up, uncleanly left behind.

While others were trying to figure out
how it all came down to holding their breaths,
by unhooking such voices from your mouth
you were becoming more one with your flesh,
searching for a state where body language
and all else there flew not towards but away,
revealing yourself through being disengaged,
which made the perfect place for you to stay.

While smitten by that soil's old histories,
with all your nights on earth as interludes
between the temperate eucalyptus trees
and explorations into something new,
you meant to keep your past an abstract speech
that aimed beyond all youthful confusions–
but soon each former vague or empty sketch
began to fill with mists of rich allusions.

If holy cities, for instance, didn't exist,
or lay hidden over those horizons,
how many able-minded physicists
would it take for them to fit on heads of pins?
When you smelled small scents of California,
retrieving once-resisted arguments,
"Yes," you'd tell them, "it's only marijuana…
No one's the sum of his stomach's contents."

In one of those deep verdant valleys, released
between high cliffs and steep ravines, you remained
as you were, stuck to your path, amplified, pleased
to be done with love's everlasting claims:
fault lines cut across the continent, arced,
like special effects in which afterglows
marked spots your dreams undid inside that dark–
where you were so much smaller than you'd known.

Secreted in Secular Orders

It's bad enough your desires
are disputed, misunderstood,
and they never wanted to hear
how you'd always start to fight
against some new communions,
thinking they couldn't be a cure,

but would anyone have guessed
that beyond that stone embrace
of a longer self-internment lay
some new sources of pleasure,
finding your consolations by
settling for such solitary joy?

The Universe

Inside it he was proud
about his settling back,
denying himself rights

to his own complexity:
the god who isn't open
to what he'd hide away

occupies a simple plot
inside a fuller garment
of singular immensity.

NOTES

Page 8: "Kanada" was the code name for the comparatively comfortable job of sorting out newly-arrived prisoners' belongings at the train stations in the Nazi death camps, ones which many "Kanadians" would survive.

Page 68: *Gris* is *grey (French); Cambio* is *Change*, as seen on signs for money-changing shops still found throughout much of Western Europe.

Books by Dos Madres Press

Mary Margaret Alvarado - *Hey Folly* (2013)

John Anson - *Jose-Maria de Heredia's Les Trophées* (2013),
　　Time Pieces - poems & translations (2014)

Jennifer Arin - *Ways We Hold* (2012)

Michael Autrey - *From The Genre Of Silence* (2008)

Stuart Bartow - *Einstein's Lawn* (2015)

Paul Bray - *Things Past and Things to Come* (2006), *Terrible Woods* (2008)

Ann Cefola - *Face Painting in the Dark* (2014)

Jon Curley - *New Shadows* (2009), *Angles of Incidents* (2012)

Grace Curtis - *The Shape of a Box* (2014)

Sara Dailey - *Earlier Lives* (2012)

Dennis Daly - *Nightwalking with Nathaniel-poems of Salem* (2014)

Richard Darabaner - *Plaint* (2012)

Deborah Diemont - *Wanderer* (2009), *Diverting Angels* (2012)

Joseph Donahue - *The Copper Scroll* (2007)

Annie Finch - *Home Birth* (2004)

Norman Finkelstein - *An Assembly* (2004), *Scribe* (2009)

Karen George - *Swim Your Way Back* (2014)

Gerry Grubbs - *Still Life* (2005), *Girls in Bright Dresses Dancing* (2010),
　　The Hive-a book we read for its honey (2013)

Richard Hague - *Burst, Poems Quickly* (2004),
　　During The Recent Extinctions (2012), *Where Drunk Men Go* (2015)

Ruth D. Handel - *Tugboat Warrior* (2013), *No Border is Perennial* (2015)

Pauletta Hansel - *First Person* (2007), *What I Did There* (2011), *Tangle* (2015)

Michael Heller - *A Look at the Door with the Hinges Off* (2006),
　　Earth and Cave (2006)

Michael Henson - *The Tao of Longing & The Body Geographic* (2010)

R. Nemo Hill - *When Men Bow Down* (2012)

W. Nick Hill - *And We'd Understand Crows Laughing* (2012)

Eric Hoffman - *Life At Braintree* (2008), *The American Eye* (2011),
　　By the Hours (2013), *Forms of Life* (2015)

85

Roald Hoffmann - *Something That Belongs To You* (2015)

James Hogan - *Rue St. Jacques* (2005)

Keith Holyoak - *My Minotaur* (2010), *Foreigner* (2012),
   The Gospel According to Judas (2015)

Nancy Kassell - *Text(isles)* (2013)

David M. Katz - *Claims of Home* (2011), *Stanzas on Oz* (2015)

Sherry Kearns - *Deep Kiss* (2013), *The Magnificence of Ruin* (2015)

Marjorie Deiter Keyishian - *Ashes and All* (2015)

Burt Kimmelman - *There Are Words* (2007), *The Way We Live* (2011)

Jill Kelly Koren - *The Work of the Body* (2015)

Ralph La Charity - *Farewellia a la Aralee* (2014)

Pamela L. Laskin - *Plagiarist* (2012)

Owen Lewis - *Sometimes Full of Daylight* (2013), *Best Man* (2015)

Richard Luftig - *Off The Map* (2006)

Austin MacRae - *The Organ Builder* (2012)

Mario Markus - *Chemical Poems-One For Each Element* (2013)

J. Morris - *The Musician, Approaching Sleep* (2006)

Patricia Monaghan - *Mary-A Life in Verse* (2014)

Rick Mullin - *Soutine* (2012), *Coelacanth* (2013),
   Sonnets on the Voyage of the Beagle (2014)

Fred Muratori - *A Civilization* (2014)

Robert Murphy - *Not For You Alone* (2004), *Life in the Ordovician* (2007),
   From Behind The Blind (2013)

Pam O'Brien - *The Answer To Each Is The Same* (2012)

Peter O'Leary - *A Mystical Theology of the Limbic Fissure* (2005)

Bea Opengart - *In The Land* (2011)

David A. Petreman - *Candlelight in Quintero-bilingual ed.* (2011)

Paul Pines - *Reflections in a Smoking Mirror* (2011),
   New Orleans Variations & Paris Ouroboros (2013),
   Fishing on the Pole Star (2014)
   Message from the Memoirist (2015)

Quanita Roberson - *Soul Growing-Wisdom for thirteen year old boys from men
   around the world* (2015)

William Schickel - *What A Woman* (2007)

Don Schofield - *In Lands Imagination Favors* (2014)

David Schloss - *Behind the Eyes* (2005), *Reports from Babylon and Beyond* (2015)

Daniel Shapiro - *The Red Handkerchief and other poems* (2014)

Murray Shugars - *Songs My Mother Never Taught Me* (2011),
     Snakebit Kudzu (2013)

Jason Shulman - *What does reward bring you but to bind you to*
     Heaven like a slave? (2013)

Maxine Silverman - *Palimpsest (2014)*

Lianne Spidel & Anne Loveland - *Pairings* (2012), *A Bird in the Hand* (2014)

Olivia Stiffler - *Otherwise, we are safe* (2013)

Carole Stone - *Hurt, the Shadow-the Josephine Hopper poems* (2013)

Nathan Swartzendruber - *Opaque Projectionist* (2009)

Jean Syed - *Sonnets* (2009)

Eileen R. Tabios - *INVENT[ST]ORY Selected Catalog Poems and New 1996-*
     2015 (2015)

Madeline Tiger - *The Atheist's Prayer* (2010), *From the Viewing Stand* (2011)

James Tolan - *Red Walls* (2011)

Brian Volck - *Flesh Becomes Word* (2013)

Henry Weinfield - *The Tears of the Muses* (2005), *Without Mythologies* (2008),
     A Wandering Aramaean (2012)

Donald Wellman - *A North Atlantic Wall* (2010),
     The Cranberry Island Series (2012)

Sarah White - *The Unknowing Muse* (2014)

Anne Whitehouse - *The Refrain* (2012)

Martin Willetts Jr. - *Secrets No One Must Talk About* (2011)

Tyrone Williams - *Futures, Elections* (2004), *Adventures of Pi* (2011)

Kip Zegers - *The Poet of Schools* (2013), *The Pond in Room 318* (2015)

www.dosmadres.com